COMMUNICATING
WITH THE
WORLD OF ISLAM

A project of the

ANNENBERG FOUNDATION TRUST
AT SUNNYLANDS

in partnership with the

HOOVER INSTITUTION

COMMUNICATING
WITH THE
WORLD OF ISLAM

Edited by

A. ROSS JOHNSON

Principal Report by

GEORGE P. SHULTZ

*Report for the
Annenberg Foundation Trust
at Sunnylands*

HOOVER INSTITUTION PRESS
Stanford University   Stanford, California

Hoover Institution Press Publication No. 556

First printing, 2008

14 13 12 11 10 09 08   9 8 7 6 5 4 3 2 1

Manufactured in the United States of America

∞ The paper used in this publication meets the minimum requirements
of the American National Standard for Information Sciences —
Permanence of Paper for Printed Library Materials, ANSI Z39.48-1992.

Library of Congress Cataloging-in-Publication Data
Communicating with the world of Islam / edited by A. Ross Johnson;
principal report by George P. Shultz; report for the Annenberg
Foundation Trust at Sunnylands.
      p. cm. — (Hoover Institution Press publication ; 556)
   ISBN-13: 978-0-8179-4822-1 (alk. paper)
      1. International broadcasting — United States. 2. Communication
in politics — Islamic countries. 3. Communication in politics —
Middle East. 4. Communicationin politics — Soviet Union —
History. 5. Radio broadcasting policy — United States. I. Johnson,
A. Ross. II. Shultz, George Pratt, 1920–
HE8697.45.U6C664   2008
384.54′4088297 — dc22   2007019824

CONTENTS

Preface

vii

Communicating with
the World of Islam

GEORGE P. SHULTZ

I

Appendix A
Dilemma of the Middle East:
Policy and Prospects for Public Diplomacy

*Rapporteur's Summary of
Rancho Mirage Seminar Discussion*

GREGORY MITROVICH

33

Appendix B
Briefing on Cold War International Broadcasting:
Lessons Learned
A. Ross Johnson and R. Eugene Parta

53

Index

69

PREFACE

This publication was inspired by discussions at a seminar, "Communicating with the Islamic World," sponsored by the Annenberg Foundation Trust at Sunnylands and held at the Lodge at Rancho Mirage, California, on February 4–6, 2005. Former Secretary of State George P. Shultz chaired the seminar, which brought together a number of other former officials responsible for public diplomacy and experts on the region. The purpose was to review key developments in the Islamic world, including attitudes toward the United States, to examine lessons learned from the success of Western broadcasting — one key element of public diplomacy — during the Cold War, and to suggest how the United States could more effectively counter extremism, promote democracy, and improve understanding of itself in the Islamic world. A rapporteur's summary of the seminar discussions is provided in Appendix A.

Communicating with the Islamic world involves a number of programs and instruments — visitorships, fellowships, area and language expertise, exhibits, publications, and broadcasting. The seminar focused primarily on broadcasting (using the term to cover all electronic media). It did not attempt to evaluate current U.S.-supported broadcasting efforts.

The Rancho Mirage seminar, and this publication, were also informed by the proceedings of an earlier conference, "Cold War Broadcasting Impact," held at the Hoover Institution, Stanford University, on October 13–15, 2004. That conference was organized by the Hoover Institution and the Cold War International History Project (CWIHP) of the Woodrow Wilson International Center for Scholars with support from The Annenberg Foundation Trust at Sunnylands and the Bernard Osher Foundation. It brought together experts from the West and from former Communist countries, veteran Western broadcasting officials, and leading former Communist officials and dissidents. The combination of new documentation from Communist-era and broadcasting archives, international expertise, and oral history provided fresh insights into a major Western instrument of the Cold War. A conference report is available from the Hoover Institution and on the CWIHP Web site: www.wilsoncenter.org/news/docs/Broadcastingconfreport 052105.doc.

A briefing on the Rancho Mirage Seminar based on the 2004 Hoover conference is provided in Appendix B.

George P. Shultz, Fouad Ajami, A. Ross Johnson, Greg Mitrovich, Abbas Milani, and R. Eugene Parta contributed to this report.

COMMUNICATING
WITH THE
WORLD OF ISLAM

Communicating with
the World of Islam

George P. Shultz

This publication seeks to answer three questions:

1. What can we learn from the broadcasting experience of the Cold War, particularly by examining the experiences of Radio Liberty, Radio Free Europe, the BBC, and the Voice of America?

2. What are current broadcasting efforts into the world of Islam and, in particular, into countries of the Arabian Peninsula, Iran, Egypt, and the Muslim communities of Europe?

3. What are the best ways of organizing U.S. efforts to communicate with the world of Islam?

LESSONS LEARNED

Drawing on a recent summary of lessons learned from the Cold War broadcasting experience,* we set out below a number of the reasons for the success of that experience, along with some discussion of those lessons.

1. Cold War broadcasting efforts were guided by a clear sense of purpose with emphasis on strategic objectives. The objectives were to constrain Soviet power (without provoking suicidal revolt), to keep alive hope of a better future, to limit tyranny, and to broaden the boundaries of internal debate, all in order to make the Soviet empire a less formidable adversary. These strategic objectives emerged after some fumbling in the early 1950s with notions of early "liberation," "rollback," and "keep[ing] the pot boiling."

---

*Provided by A. Ross Johnson and R. Eugene Parta and included in full as Appendix B. The lessons identified here emerged from papers and discussions at the conferences mentioned in the Preface. Conference participants had studied the records of Radio Liberty and Radio Free Europe, now located at the Hoover Institution; had been part of the effort of the Radios and of Voice of America and the BBC; or were at the receiving end of the broadcasts in one capacity or another.

2. Methods for appraising effectiveness were developed to guide fiscal allocations, but even more importantly, to suggest new ways of going about the effort.

3. A strong capability for sophisticated appraisal of the adversary was developed and a cadre of specialized researchers with deep area expertise was assembled. This information and analysis function was not envisaged at the outset; it was developed at Radio Free Europe (RFE) and Radio Liberty (RL) over time in response to operational need. It became in turn a major contributor to U.S. government and scholarly analyses.

4. Differentiated and tailored programs were developed for multiple audiences among and within target countries. Balanced world and regional news was a staple for all audiences. Programs for Communist elites included coverage of conflicts within and among Communist parties and reports on social democracy in Europe. Programs for non-Communist elites covered Western culture and intellectual life and, as internal dissent developed, amplification of that dissent. Programs for general audiences covered everything from agriculture to religion to labor to sports. Banned

Western and internal music was featured. Willis Conover of Voice of America (VOA) introduced a generation of Russians and Poles to jazz; the RFE Hungarian Service "Teenager Party" program attracted a generation of Hungarian youth to RFE; and Western music attracted listeners in the other RFE target countries as well. In the USSR, the *magnitizdat* phenomenon introduced banned Soviet underground music to a wide public.

5. The programs were purposeful, responsible, and relevant to their audiences, and a great effort was made to develop their credibility. Events of the day were covered, but thematic programming was important as well (e.g., a series on parliamentary institutions in a democracy). Commentary was included along with straight news and news analysis, and audiences were attracted to star-quality commentators. It was essential that programs built and maintained credibility by reporting the bad news along with the good, as in coverage of Watergate and Vietnam. Responsible programming was, at its best, calm in tone and, after the early 1950s, it avoided transmitting tactical advice and, especially, any encouragement of violent resistance. Programming emphasized local developments and was attuned to the listeners through constant au-

dience feedback obtained from traveler surveys and listener mail, and through continuous management of quality control.

6. The broadcast organizations believed in decentralization and in a large measure of autonomy for country broadcast units. This led to wider audiences and to the improvement and quality that typically stem from competition.

7. The broadcasts were accompanied by multiple-media operations beginning with balloon leaflets in the 1950s, and later including periodicals, Western books, and locally unpublished texts.

8. Funding was provided by Congress at levels that were adequate without being lavish and was subject to careful fiscal oversight.

9. Distance and insulation from official government policies were sustained and a tradition of journalistic independence nourished. The authorizing legislation, Section 2 of the Board for International Broadcasting Act of 1973, provided for "an independent broadcast media, operating in a manner not inconsistent with the broad foreign policy objectives of the United States and in accordance with high professional standards," giving RFE and RL considerable

journalistic flexibility. Advocacy of specific U.S. policies was not required and was, in fact, avoided. The BBC enjoyed similar autonomy in the British context. VOA's journalistic independence, affirmed in 1976 by law in the VOA Charter, was sometimes challenged by administration policy interference and complicated by the requirement to broadcast administration policy editorials.

10. The target audiences lived in an "information poor" environment subject to continual propaganda and censorship, which created receptive listeners, a key ingredient for success. East Europeans, in particular, felt especially cut off from the rest of Europe and were predominantly pro-American.

11. The participation of émigrés in broadcasts was handled carefully. This was no simple task because émigrés frequently exaggerate both positive and negative news. Nevertheless, the Cold War experience showed that it is possible and important to use known figures who are fluent in the language of the country in which a program is broadcast.

12. A flow of events offered opportunities because people denied information by propaganda sources are generally eager to know what is going on. Cherno-

byl is an interesting example because the endangered population got all its initial news about the event from the West and either nothing or a distorted view from the Soviets. Credibility makes it possible for broadcasters to take full advantage of these events.

In brief, Western broadcasts had a remarkable impact in the USSR and Eastern Europe during the Cold War. They reached mass audiences, as documented by traveler surveys at the time and confirmed now by evidence from the formerly closed Communist archives. And they reached essential elites, both within the Communist regimes and among regime opponents. The main keys to the mass and elite audiences were the credibility and relevance of the broadcasts. Government mechanisms were geared to providing public funding and oversight while ensuring management autonomy and journalistic independence.

Current Efforts

The United States and other Western countries currently support a variety of broadcasting efforts (including radio, television, and Internet Web sites) to the Middle East. As distinct from the Cold War period, however, there is a plethora of indigenous TV and radio broadcasting, more in some countries than others. New radio and TV indigenous initiatives keep appearing. This represents the competition or, in some cases, an opportunity to make common cause in some manner, but it represents a much more complex problem than the Cold War problem.

The following listing, though certainly not exhaustive, captures a great deal of what the United States* and other Western countries are broadcasting in the Middle East. We limit ourselves here to a listing; details may be found in the publications and Web sites of the various broadcasters. In the Arabic language, the United States currently supports Radio Sawa, RFE/RL's Radio Free Iraq, and Al Hurra Television. The BBC World Service broadcasts in Arabic throughout the Middle East. Deutsche Welle has Arab-language radio and television programs. Other Arab-language international broadcasters include Kol Israel and French-sponsored Radio Monte Carlo.

In the Persian language, the United States supports

*Since the passage of the International Broadcasting Act in 1994, all U.S. international broadcasting is under the direction of the Broadcasting Board of Governors (an Executive Branch agency headed by eight governors of both parties nominated by the president and confirmed by the Senate and the Secretary of State). The BBG is intended to insulate the broadcasting entities from U.S. government pressure. Information on the BBG and the broadcasters it oversees is available at www.bbg.gov.

Radio Farda, Voice of America radio, and Voice of America television. Other Persian-language international broadcasters include the BBC, China Radio International, Deutsche Welle, Kol Israel, NHK Radio Japan, Radio France International, and Voice of Russia.

The United States also supports a number of RFE/RL and VOA programs in the languages of Afghanistan and Pakistan: Uzbek, Kurdish, Dari, Pashto, and Urdu. The BBC broadcasts in Pashto, Uzbek, and Urdu. Deutsche Welle broadcasts in Afghan languages.

Various privately run endeavors exist as well. Los Angeles has a large Iranian community, and there are numerous stations run by expatriates that broadcast satellite TV programs to Iran. Layalina Productions, started in March 2002, is a private, non-profit corporation dedicated to creating informational and entertaining television programming to bridge the divide between the Arab Middle East and the United States.

FUTURE DIRECTIONS

In this section we survey briefly the current state of the Arab world and Iran, and then consider how the experience in Cold War broadcasting can be applied to current efforts to influence the world of Islam.

*The Arab Lands**

The United States is involved in a critical struggle against a complex movement of radical Islam that uses the tactics of terror in an effort to change the way the world works. U.S. military and economic efforts to deal with this problem are a necessary but not sufficient condition for success. As President Bush said in his 2005 inaugural address, "In the long-term, the peace we seek will only be achieved by eliminating the conditions that feed radicalism and ideologies of murder. If whole regions of the world remain in despair and grow in hatred, they will be the recruiting grounds for terror, and that terror will stalk America and other free nations for decades. The only force powerful enough to stop the rise of tyranny and terror, and replace hatred with hope, is the force of human freedom."

There is a canon nowadays that dwells on the rampant anti-Americanism in Arab and Muslim lands. The pollsters—the Pew survey, the Zogby survey, and others—return from those lands with what have become predictable results: huge majorities in Pakistan, Jordan, Egypt, and Saudi Arabia proclaim an uncompromising anti-Americanism. Those results are then inserted into our national debate, and the received

---

*This section is based on a draft by Fouad Ajami.

wisdom is that the anti-Americanism has been triggered by America's war against terror, by our toppling of the Saddam Hussein regime in Iraq, and by the continuing Arab-Israeli conflict. This political judgment can be questioned, and there is a whole different way of reading this anti-Americanism. "They hate us, what's wrong with us?" ought to yield to another way of framing this large question: "They hate us, what's eating at their societies?" In critically important societies in the "broader Middle East," anti-Americanism is the diet that rulers provide for populations denied a role in the making of a decent public order. "Nations follow the religion of their kings," goes an Arabic maxim. The anti-Americanism in some Muslim lands is part of the rulers' strategy, an expression of the revolt against modernism plaguing Islamic societies today.

In freedom's confrontation with the Communist world, our broadcasting aimed at, and found, populations eager for an alternative source of information to compete with the official "truth." The Arab-Muslim world today presents a different challenge. This world is "wired" in the extreme, its public life a tumult of arguments and messages, its underemployed young people prey to the satellite channels, to the radical preachers, and to the steady drumbeats of anti-Americanism. A strategy to reach these populations would have to acknowledge the difficulty of this terrain.

The American dilemma is particularly acute in Arab and

Muslim societies supposedly in our strategic orbit—Saudi Arabia, Egypt, Pakistan and Jordan come to mind. In the words of the distinguished historian Bernard Lewis, these lands could be described as pro-American regimes with anti-American populations. They contrast with Iran, where the rulers are anti-American but the population is on the other side. In the two most important Arab countries—Saudi Arabia and Egypt—the ground is treacherous. These two countries, it is fair to say, gave us Al Qaeda and the death pilots of 9/11. It is from the "deep structure" of these two societies that the modern phenomenon of Islamist terrorism emerged. Starkly put, the disaffected children of these two countries came together to strike at America as part of their campaign to bring down their entrenched regimes. A ruthlessly brilliant man of the upper reaches of Egyptian society, the physician Ayman al-Zawahiri, distinguished between what he called "the near enemy" (the Arab regimes), and "the distant enemy" (the United States). The terror against America was the choice made because our country was open and unaware of the dangers stalking it; because the Islamists could slip through our open borders, exploiting liberty and constitutional limits.

The Saudi and Egyptian custodians of power know that America was caught in the crossfire between themselves and their Islamists, but they never own up to it. They play with us a double-game: they provide us with some intelligence and access to their workings, and to the ways of their networks of terror, while scapegoating their domestic troubles by nurturing a culture and a public information system poisoned by a malignant anti-Americanism. You need only read *Al-Ahram*, President Hosni Mubarak's principal newspaper, to be treated to the ceaseless anti-Americanism and conspiracy theories. Likewise with the press and with the religious pulpits of Saudi Arabia. The Wahhabi hatred of modernism is fierce, and anti-Americanism now suffuses that country's life. There are thousands of liberal/secularist Saudis, many of them educated by our elite universities, but they are hunkered down and terrified, and, frankly, they don't see us as their friends. In their world, American power is tethered to the ruling dynasty, and this embattled minority is in a no-man's-land.

Our leaders know the depth, and the danger, of these two Arab settings. In both his seminal speech to the National Endowment for Democracy in November 2003 and in his State of the Union Address of 2005, President Bush spoke to, and of, these problematic allies in Riyadh and Cairo: "The government of Saudi Arabia can demonstrate its leadership in the region by expanding the role of its people in determining their future. And the proud nation of Egypt, which showed the way toward peace in the

Middle East, can now show the way toward democracy in the Middle East." We have been trying to wean these two nations away from their authoritarian ways. But these two regimes, it must be conceded, have been good at feeding the forces of anti-Americanism while cooperating with America in the shadows. A terrible price has been paid in the process: the modernist possibilities have been damaged in these two lands, and we, for our part, have paid dearly for dangers that came our way from purported allies.

Egypt is a proud nation, to be sure. But its pride stands in sharp relief against the background of dismal political, economic, and cultural results. Egypt's standing has eroded on all the indices that matter—political freedom, economic advance, transparency in economic and public life. Fairly or not, we are implicated in the deeds of the Mubarak regime. This is our second-largest recipient of foreign aid, but the aid has been squandered, and Egypt is in the throes of a deep political crisis. From Egypt, we hear a steady mix of anti-Americanism, anti-Semitism, and anti-modernism. Our embassy there has been caught up in an ongoing clash with the media and with the organs of the regime. What is said about America in that crowded and important country is a betrayal of the American aid given to Egypt. We have not been good at reaching Egyptians, or at challenging the conspiracy theories that have become a staple of their public life. We need to break out of this unhealthy embrace of the Egyptian regime. This is a pan-Arab matter, for Egyptians — in the main embittered, angry, and disappointed in their country — have turned on us in all arenas. They expressed no remorse for the terrors of 9/11, they opposed the Iraq war, and both the regime and the "civil society" were remarkably hostile to the Iraqi people's attempt to rid themselves of the legacy of Saddam Hussein's tyranny.

In Saudi Arabia, the challenge is equally daunting. Powered with a new windfall — in 2004, Saudi Arabia took in $110 billion in oil income — public life in that country is filled with a belligerent kind of piety. The religion is made to carry and express the revolt against reason, a determination to frighten the liberal minority within the land, and to spread Wahhabism's influence abroad. The regime has manipulated this religious bigotry, allowed it ample running room, and given it access to the mosques and to the religious institutions and philanthropies. But of late, there has been something of a retreat from this policy on the part of the House of Saud. The extremists have brought the fight onto Saudi soil. The tranquility of the realm has been shattered, and with it the smug belief that Arabia was immune to sedition and troubles. It must be this re-assessment that accounts for the new moderation of the Saudi-owned satellite television news channel Al-Arabiya (based in Dubai) and of the influential newspaper *Asharq Al-Awsat*. (The former is owned by in-laws of the late King Fahd, while the latter is the property of King Fahd's full brother, Prince Salman, and presided over by Salman's son, Prince Faisal.) The Saudis may just be awakening to the monster of radicalism that they had fed and let loose on others.

These Arab and Muslim countries need to be monitored, and known as they are. We need able linguists and interpreters. We need to persist with the message, so forcefully stated by President Bush, that we stand for liberty and that we believe that liberty can flourish on Arab and Muslim soil. Our enemies (Iran, Syria, the rogues) need to be told this as often, and as forcefully, as our friends in Egypt and Saudi Arabia. For decades, we have accepted a terrible bargain with Arab and Muslim authoritarianism. On 9/11 we discovered that the bargain did not work. A public diplomacy worth the effort and the price tag must start from that recognition. Its message must be free of any debilitating guilt. We have to state in unequivocal terms our belief in the necessity of modernity in Muslim lands. We must let the rulers and their circles of power know that we are listening in on them, that we are in the know as to the sort of things they say on their television channels and in their papers and in their pulpits. We might be surprised to find out that the tone changes in those lands once people are put on notice that we have shed our innocence, and that we are no longer taken in by their dissimulation.

Much of what has been said about the impact of the Iraq war on America's standing in Arab lands is off the mark. Beyond the headlines of roadside bombs and daily carnage, there is a vibrant media culture in Iraq today. By one estimate, there are more than 250 daily and weekly papers in Iraq; there is a multiplicity of private radio and television stations in Baghdad and in the other provinces. There is no censorship of the media. This is a healthy contrast to the servile press in neighboring Syria, Egypt, Jordan, and Saudi Arabia. We are slowly — and painfully at times — winning this bet on freedom in Iraq. It is their world, and they will have to do most of the repair. But our power and support matter greatly, as does the optimistic and uplifting message articulated by President Bush that we will not consign the Arabs to the "soft bigotry of low expectations."

We need to develop — by example, and with our support — the middle ground between the media of incitement (Al Jazeera) and the servile media of the Arab regimes. Al Jazeera is now nearly a decade old. It caters to "the street" and to popular passions. It has its audience, and it always will. But doubts have arisen about its brand of journalism. There is distrust of it among Iraqis and among Lebanese because the satellite channel does not support their quest for freedom. The taste for the spectacular may have peaked, and credible journalism could make a dent on the Arab psyche.

*Iran**

The case of Iran offers challenges and promises different from those in the Arab world. Historically, Iranians have seen themselves as distinct from Arabs and dislike being lumped together with them. Furthermore, the reality on the ground in Iran today makes the country different from the rest of the Muslim Middle East. The biggest difference is that the people of Iran seem to be overwhelmingly pro-American and pro-democracy while the unelected mullahs who rule them see virulent anti-Americanism as part of their *raison d'être*.

The delicacy of the U.S. position lies precisely in the fact that while it must work to curtail Iran's ambitions for nuclear weapons, it must not, in the short run, seem to be making a "deal" that legitimizes the regime.

The powerful democratic movement in Iran, now in temporary tactical retreat as the result of the failures of the Khatami experience and the last "election," is sure to stir back into full action at some unpredictable moment in the future. The United States can help bring about that "moment" and, at the same time, must begin planning for how to help the transition to democracy when the moment comes.

In navigating our way to a solid public diplomacy strat-

*This section is based on a draft by Abbas Milani.

egy on Iran, we must have a clear and sober analysis of our friends and foes in Iran, including their relative strengths and weaknesses. The Iranian democratic movement, the middle class that is its backbone, and the urban women who have spearheaded it for the past quarter of a century are the strategic allies of the United States. The Iranian youth who constitute close to 60 percent of the population are predominantly pro-democratic and pro-Western, and thus form part of the embryonic pro-American grand alliance for democracy. Many members of the Iranian industrial entrepreneurial group have been trained in the West; they are by and large pro-American and are wary of the regime's corruption, incompetence, and adventurism. They want a thriving private sector, a thinning role for the state, an end to corruption and crony capitalism, an end to the embargo, extended economic ties with the United States, and, more than anything else, the rule of law. They, too, are our allies. More and more of the urban poor and elements of the Iranian countryside are beginning to lose what little faith they had in the system. The economically powerful Iranian Diaspora in the United States wants democracy in Iran and can help underwrite the cost of the transition to democracy. More importantly, they can be a helpful resource in fine-tuning the way we talk to the Iranian population. We must find ways to strengthen the democratic movement by bringing together these disparate forces while at the same time not giving the mullahs an excuse to attack or muzzle them.

In talking with the Iranian people, we must keep in mind both strategic as well as tactical goals and tools. As in the days of the Cold War, we need to use every tool and weapon in our arsenal. These include publishing magazines that promote democracy, supporting publishing houses that contribute to the strengthening of a democratic dialogue, organizing conferences that deal with issues relating to democracy in Iran, and finally helping establish a 21st-century media to speak with the Iranian people that includes short-wave and medium-wave radio and television, radio pod-casting, and the Internet, all dedicated to the promotion of democracy in Iran. We need to use language free from the taint of hectoring or condescension and commensurate with the sophisticated democratic discourse that has recently evolved in Iran. What works in Egypt or Saudi Arabia does not necessarily work in Iran. In each case, the message and the medium must fit the intended recipients. The thousands of exiled Iranian intellectuals can help fashion a language that best suits Iran.

Iran today is unusually well "wired"; it is the country with the most bloggers — some 75,000 — after Brazil and the United States. There is also a nascent movement in the use of radio pod-casting — personal computers used for private, Internet-accessible radios. In addition, of the country's

75 million people, some 20 million have access to satellite dishes that connect them to the outside world and to the Iranian Diaspora media. That leaves another 55 million who are without access, and they hold the key to the future success of the pro-American democratic coalition.

However, the Diaspora media has failed to mobilize the masses and has gradually lost its credibility as a reliable source of news. The United States can help ignite the democratic movement by providing technological assistance through medium- and short-wave access that allows the great majority of Iranians to participate in what can become, even in its initial phase, the virtual community of the democratic coalition. Pope John Paul's journey to Poland in 1979 ignited the country's democratic movement by conveying to the millions of Poles who had come to greet the Pontiff that they were not alone. In Iran today, an expanded and expert media presence with a honed message that reaches every corner of the country could play the same unifying role. It could convey news about the democratic movement, expose the corruption and despotism of the regime, and inform the masses of the real news of the country and of the world.

Aside from these strategic considerations, the United States can also make a number of short-term tactical gestures that will disarm the regime's anti-American rhetoric and strengthen the hands of the democratic movement.

Here are two examples:

1. Put an immediate end to the embargo on the import of earthquake warning equipment. Iran sits on some of the world's most dangerous faults and the Islamic regime has been reckless in doing absolutely nothing about this danger. It is estimated that the Iranian capital, Tehran, would lose close to two million people in a future quake. Donating some of this equipment would not only expose the regime's dangerous dereliction of duty but also would improve the image of the United States in Iran and the rest of the Muslim world.

2. Provide detailed programs that show the real costs and dangers of Iran's nuclear program and underscore the fact that acquiring nuclear bombs may prolong the life of the regime.

Influencing the World of Islam

The malady in the Arab lands and Iran thus understood, here are some thoughts about how to undertake the task of influencing the world of Islam in a positive direction:

1. Broadcast and provide information. Lessons of the Cold War experience show that international broadcasting and associated information methods can have

an important impact and play a significant role in dealing with the problem. The task is much more complicated in this case because the target audience is so diverse and the competition for attention is so large. Nevertheless, the mission is essential and the job can be done.

2. Construct a realistic sense of mission. While radical Islam is, in a sense, the problem, the mission needs to focus on helping what may be called mainstream Muslims address the issues and take on the radicals. In the end, it is the Islamic community itself that needs to engage in this battle and we need to encourage that effort. In doing so, we advance the spread of freedom and democracy, and we encourage the regimes to provide good and responsive governance for their people. We also know that radical Islamists cannot function without a surrounding population that acquiesces in, or can be frightened into, supporting or not opposing them. So our effort has to be to dry up the sea of support in which terrorists swim. That is the mission.

3. Build a credible case for the necessity of the effort. Outline in broad terms what needs to be done and thereby attract the funds that will draw high talent to the effort, will assure sustainability, and will allow for considerable variety in what is undertaken.

4. Study the target audiences carefully. We will need to differentiate among them. Words like "Arabs" or "Muslims" are deceptive because they conceal immense variety. Above all, pay attention to women, who in some countries* are kept out of everyday life and have huge amounts of time to watch TV at home where the morals police can't get at them. Women's content programming is essential. Something similar, but with very different content, should be designed for another vast audience, unemployed males who sit around at the corner coffeehouses all day.

5. Beyond the broad sweep of programs such as those now sponsored by the U.S. government, make special efforts to target audiences in Saudi Arabia, Egypt, Iran, the Muslim communities in Western Europe, and possibly Pakistan. The history of radical movements shows that a high proportion of them originate in one form or another in these areas.

6. Include both U.S. government and outside efforts. Unfortunately, proficiency in languages and efforts at area studies have declined in the United States. Current Mideast Studies programs are inadequate. A

---

*The daily lives of women vary greatly in Arab countries, e.g., Lebanon and Egypt versus Saudi Arabia.

major effort is necessary to encourage universities to undertake scholarship in this field and to preserve and enhance all the ways in which the relevant languages are acquired by at least a reasonable number of Americans.

7. Monitor what people say and be ready to interact. Much of what passes for commentary is altogether delusional. The Middle East, always remember, is the world center for conspiracy theories. So some sort of counter-conspiracy desk is needed. If we are candid, open, and factually correct, we have a platform for countering some of this delusional talk. Much of the world of Islam has lost contact with reality, with the relationship of cause to effect. Reality needs to be a centerpiece in what we talk about.

8. As part of the effort to connect people with reality, place emphasis on the importance and the virtues of work. Among the problems in the European Muslim community is the fact that, as estimated for some urban areas, well over half the men of Moroccan origin over the age of forty were living on welfare of one kind or another and had little expectation of working. Work connects people with reality.

9. We need to think through the problem of addressing the Muslim populations in Western Europe, espe-

cially, though not exclusively, those in Britain, France, the Netherlands, and Germany. We will need close collaboration with the governments involved but we need to approach them with ideas of our own. We might ask ourselves, "How do we deal with intolerant and violent forces in a tolerant society?" and "How do we encourage sensible Muslim voices to rise above the intolerant barrage?"

10. We also need to develop ideas and approaches to Saudi Arabia, Egypt, and Iran. Each is different.

11. Develop means of evaluating the effects of our efforts. This is essential in maintaining funding but also in the constant process of honing our messages so that they are as effective as possible.

12. Encourage differentiated programs that are broadly consistent with the worldview of the United States and allow for decentralized creativity in efforts to reach various populations and in developing ways of putting messages. In this connection, émigrés can be very helpful, but they need to be evaluated with great care. Émigrés tend to exaggerate the positive and the negative, but really credible individuals can be identified and they can carry great weight when they speak because, among other reasons, they manage the language in a natural way.

13. Although governmental efforts are the centerpiece in all of this, private efforts can be helpful. As a first example, Layalina Productions, mentioned earlier, is developing program content under the leadership of former ambassador Richard Fairbanks. The idea is to air these programs on existing and watched stations. This effort deserves support. A second example is that generated by a group of advertising people on behalf of a number of companies operating overseas. Their work stems from a salesman's incentive to get people abroad to like Americans and, therefore, their products. That is a goal certainly compatible with U.S. government objectives.

14. Put emphasis on the importance of education in the basic sense of the word. Too much of what passes for education in the world of Islam is simply propaganda and doesn't prepare people adequately for tasks of work and tasks of critical evaluation of what they are hearing. Special incentives might be developed to encourage people to learn the English language.

15. There are many voices in the Arab world that carry encouraging and reasonable messages, often with an effort to legitimize themselves by including some critical comments about America. We should not

worry excessively about the attacks on us. We should work with the positive words of these voices and amplify them.

16. No matter how impressive our effort, it will never succeed so long as Arab regimes continue to pump out tons of daily propaganda that over recent decades has driven ordinary Arabs into a perpetual condition of hyper-inflamed rage at outsiders, thus diverting the Arab populations away from the regimes themselves. A concerted effort is needed on this problem. We need to maintain the pressure on the rulers of Qatar over the content and programming of Al Jazeera. They own it and finance it, and, by recent credible reports, the Emir of Qatar and his principal aides have been made to understand by the Administration that they can't befriend us while sponsoring this brand of journalism.

17. Consider including in our media strategy material that deftly shows that the Arab-Islamic world needs to communicate with us in a far better way than they have done. Such material could show how objectionable they look to the world when they appear to be saturated in hate, self-pity, and slaughter.

18. Our news content must be candid, tuned to local audiences, and remorselessly accurate. Credibility will emerge, and credibility is the name of the game. Major events come along (the elections in Iraq, the Cedar Revolution), and credibility leads people to take our reports on such events as accurate. In the process, we discipline all the other outlets.

APPENDIX A

Dilemma of the Middle East:
Policy and Prospects for Public Diplomacy

Summary of Rancho Mirage
Seminar Discussions

GREGORY MITROVICH

(seminar rapporteur)

We can overcome our difficulties in communicating with
the Middle East by effectively using public diplomacy, including international broadcasting, but we must first iden-
tify the key obstacles to our policies in the region, recognizing that the area presents far more of a challenge to our

---

*The seminar was convened with the understanding that the proceedings
would be published but not attributed to individual participants. This di-
gest is intended to provide an overview of the discussions without attempting to capture all differences among participants. Not all participants agreed with all the points in this summary.

public diplomacy strategies than our previous experiences with broadcasting behind the Iron Curtain. To effectively communicate, we must consider four significant differences: the Middle East is largely populated by pro-American regimes and anti-American populations; it is an information-rich setting where international broadcasting must successfully compete with a myriad of other media; the rapid pace of technological development is constantly reshaping regional communication; and it is an environment rife with rumor and conspiracy thinking — conditions that are largely the reverse of what Western broadcasters faced in confronting Soviet propaganda behind the Iron Curtain.

LESSONS FROM THE PAST

Before we can examine the Middle East in greater depth we require a better understanding of the "lessons learned" from Western broadcasting to the Soviet Bloc during the Cold War. Our efforts to foster democratic change and counter anti-Americanism in the Islamic World — strikingly similar to our broadcasting objectives for the Soviet Bloc — will benefit greatly from this effort.

New research has concluded that Western broadcasts had a remarkable impact in the USSR and Eastern Europe.

They reached both mass audiences and key elites within the Communist regimes and among regime opponents. Those audiences tuned in for an alternative to state-controlled news, for information about positive developments in other countries, and for hope that a better life was possible. The keys to reaching and building large-scale mass and elite audiences were:

1. Broadcasting reliability, established by a track record of truthful and accurate news.

2. Use of carefully selected émigré broadcasters, some of whom were celebrities within the target countries, operating within decentralized broadcasting organizations under essential American management and "quality control".

3. Understanding target country developments and audiences through information collection and analytical and media research.

4. Developing differentiated and tailored programs for multiple audiences among and within the target countries. Programming covered events of the day (e.g., the Chernobyl nuclear plant disaster) and also key democracy themes (e.g., series on civil rights in the U.S.; civilian control of the military; basic human rights; free market economies). Continuous audience feedback ensured long-term programming relevance.

5. Developing mechanisms geared to providing public funding and oversight while ensuring management autonomy and journalistic independence.

6. Providing complementary Western broadcasts including RFE/RL, VOA, BBC, and other broadcasters, each with a different emphasis and "value-added".

7. Articulating a clear purpose that earned bipartisan support in successive administrations and the Congress, ensuring adequate sustained funding.

8. Broadcasting programs that conformed to broad American national security strategy but were separated from day-to-day policy considerations.

Our Cold War efforts would not have succeeded had the United States not committed significant resources to public diplomacy. However, all recent studies of current American public diplomacy agree that it is severely under-funded and has lacked effective leadership for years. The Djerejian Commission report* is one of a number of such studies offering a systematic inventory of the problems and a comprehensive set of recommendations to overcome them. It

*Changing Minds; Winning Peace. Report of the Advisory Group on Public Diplomacy for the Arab and Muslim World [Djerejian Commission]. October 2003, Executive Summary, pp. 8–10; Specific Recommendations, pp. 69–71. http://www.state.gov/documents/organization/24882.pdf.

bluntly states that our existing programs are wholly inadequate given our present-day difficulties. Below is a brief summary of the current state of affairs throughout the Middle East.

ANTI-AMERICANISM IN THE MIDDLE EAST

The rise of anti-American sentiments on the Arab street, and thus much of our current difficulties, is partly traceable to a pro-Israeli shift in United States policy after the 1967 war. Prior to the Israeli victory and the subsequent occupation of the West Bank and the Sinai, American policymakers had been more balanced in their relations between Israel and Arab countries, but shifted to a more pro-Israeli policy in its aftermath. The end of the Cold War only accentuated this trend. The cause of this shift reflected, in part, the growing democratization of American foreign policy and the increased role for political pressure groups. Additionally, the demise of the Soviet Union removed the ever-present fear that drove much of U.S. policy in the Middle East: that Arab oil supplies would be lost to the West.

Consequently, Arab publics feel neglected by the United States, have recently come to sense a lack of U.S. commitment to resolving the Israeli-Palestinian conflict, and have concluded that U.S. administrations focus on the region solely during times of crisis. With the end of the Cold War, the ensuing budget cuts coupled with the end of the United States Information Agency gravely weakened the U.S. public diplomacy apparatus. Rightly or wrongly, the Arab street has come to believe that America cares little for its plight — a sentiment that extremist forces have exploited to their advantage.

Arab populations are prepared to engage in activities — even negative ones — to re-engage America in the peace process, even though these activities may have seriously detrimental consequences for them. One example is support for Saddam Hussein. Arabs understood that he was a murderous tyrant, but Saddam challenged the United States and thus forced the U.S. to concentrate much of its Middle East policy on him. So, too, today with Osama bin Laden and the 9/11 attacks. Consequently, while the majority of these populations aspire to democracy and hope that the experiment begun in Iraq will succeed, they also take some satisfaction in seeing the United States bloodied and battered in the process. Not every Arab maintains these beliefs; many oppose Islamic fundamentalism but as yet do not feel any need to support American causes, and thus represent a very silent majority.

The political problems we face in the Middle East are aggravated by numerous social, economic, and demographic trends. First, the region is bereft of democracy and burdened by corrupt regimes whose poor performances have devastated the region. Second, the failure of the Pan-Arab nationalist movements of the 1950s has led to an estrangement among Arab communities and a feeling that their current governments are too subservient to the United States. Third, the region is plagued with economic and social stagnation caused by too much state control of the economy coupled with pervasive corruption and an over-reliance on oil. The legacy of socialism has resulted in a population that expects everything from the regime. Fourth, the region suffers from an extremely high birthrate that strains social and political institutions. Fifth, education levels are exceptionally poor and are often heavily focused on religious training. The result is that schools across the Middle East are graduating students with negligible practical skills and with little hope of finding employment.

What, then, is to be done? Some believe that the region finds itself in the same condition as Western Europe during the Middle Ages and that only a "renaissance" can arouse the Middle East from its current despair. Yet today it is the Islamists who dominate the intellectual high ground, followed by large numbers of traditionalists who are opposed to what they see as illegitimate, non-Islamic philosophies seeking to control the region. There are as yet very few reformers who are willing to openly preach the virtues of modernity and who strive to defeat its opponents. There was hope that immigration to Western Europe and the impact of living in a highly developed society would increase support for modernism within Arab society. Unfortunately, the reverse has come true. Arab populations, even those born and raised in Western Europe, feel alienated from Western society and gravitate toward Arab ghettos often centered on the mosque, where their feelings of estrangement are exploited by radical Muslim clerics.

Much of the Arab world's anti-American sentiments reflect these feelings of alienation within Muslim society. Yet their virulence can also be traced to the egregious abuse of these sentiments by ostensibly pro-American regimes that hope to channel their own peoples' hatred of them against the United States. They seek to take advantage of the envy American prosperity and innovation has engendered in these populations, and Middle Eastern regimes abuse these feelings in order to vent the hatred of the Arab street away from their dictatorships. These states are not interested in democracy and do everything in their power to suppress political debate. The governments realize that their populations have grown frustrated, and believe that they can reduce the threat to themselves by directing these disaffections towards the United States. Therefore, we must consider carefully what anti-Americanism actually means. Does it mean, literally, that the Arab world hates America, or is it a reflection of their own feelings about themselves and their current status? Questions have been raised about the interpretation of the Zogby and Pew Research surveys that indicate that favorable attitudes toward the United States have plummeted to negligible levels. Designers of these polls should confront critics within the Middle East area studies profession who question their methods and challenge their conclusions.

Regardless of the effectiveness of public opinion polling, we face the uncertainty that our efforts to reduce anti-Americanism may in the end have little effect, as a central source of its existence is the battle between the forces of stagnation and modernism within the Arab world—a fight that must be won by the modernists within the Middle East.

IRAN: DANGER AND OPPORTUNITY

Iran presents us with circumstances that are quite the opposite of what we face in the Arab world—an anti-American government with a population sympathetic to America and supportive of its ideals. Recognizing this difference as well as the many complexities that underlie life in revolutionary Iran is crucial if we are to develop a successful public diplomacy strategy for Iran.

The rulers of the Islamic Republic consider recent events to have significantly strengthened their position in the Middle East and provided them with greater leverage in their confrontation with the United States. The insurgency in Iraq has tied down over 150,000 U.S. troops in a commitment that might last for years, thus precluding serious military pressure against Tehran. Their religious brethren, the Shia, will dominate the new Iraqi government, and along with their allies in Syria, Iranian leaders believe they have effectively encircled and outmaneuvered the United States in the region. Through astute use of their oil assets, they have successfully nullified the most significant threat to their regime: UN sanctions in response to their burgeoning nuclear program. Recent deals with China have practically guaranteed a veto of any Security Council resolutions authorizing sanctions against Iran. Iran's mullahs are so confident in the strength and stability of their position that they openly disparage the United States in a manner unlike any since the revolution. Consequently, the danger from the Islamic Republic has rapidly escalated and threatens both the Middle East and the world.

The development of a nuclear capability by Iran poses one of the most critical long-term challenges for the United States. Iranian leaders consider possession of the bomb the key to their survival — a guarantee that they will not follow in the footsteps of Saddam Hussein. Rather, leading Iranian clerics openly admit that they intend to follow, instead, in the footsteps of North Korea, whose nuclear program — they believe — has made it immune to U.S. pressures. Iran's leaders learned from Saddam Hussein's failure and have developed a two-front approach to ensure the ultimate success of their program. First, they have effectively negated the military options available to the United States by cleverly dividing the program into numerous parts spread across the country and often located within urban areas to ensure significant loss of civilian life if attacked. Thus a replay of the Israelis' preemptive strike against Iraq's Osirak reactor is out of the question. Second, by enticing Security Council members with lucrative contacts in both oil and nuclear power, they have realistically ensured a veto of any potential Security Council resolution calling for sanctions. Oil contracts with China and India, a nuclear power agreement with Russia, and the prospect of similar economic opportunities for Europeans have enticed some members of the Security Council to resist the imposition of sanctions on Iran. The mullahs of Iran believe that they have checkmated the United States.

Iran's domestic picture, however, provides a powerful ray of hope for U.S. policymakers and for avenues for public diplomacy. Some polling data and an extensive amount of anecdotal evidence suggest that the United States is quite popular with the Iranian people. Iranians admire and respect America because the United States has for so long stood for the Iranian people against the regime. Conversely, Western Europe, China, and Russia are despised for sacrificing the interests of Iran's population for their own economic benefit.

Polling data also paint a far more precarious situation for the ruling leadership than the mullahs are willing to admit. Disintegration of the Iranian economy, rampant corruption, and the yearning of the Iranian people for elements of Western and, in particular, American culture, have led to an almost universal disdain for the current domestic order. A Gallup poll several years ago that surveyed several thousand Iranians concluded that ninety percent of the Iranian population is opposed to the status quo. The regime responded by imprisoning several of the pollsters.

Cracks are developing as well within the Iranian leadership. The Revolutionary Guard wants a share of power and wealth in Iran, and is exploiting its station to enrich itself. In recent years a number of Revolutionary Guard leaders have become millionaires through the Guard's control over key customs posts. They have also obtained lucrative contracts for construction projects throughout the country. Yet there are others within the Revolutionary Guard who are beginning to express dissatisfaction with the state of the country. The former deputy head of the Revolutionary Guard has defected with the hope of leading the opposition against the mullahs. Other reports indicate that even within the religious leadership, differences over the role of clerics in government have strained relations among the mullahs, even at the level of Grand Ayatollah. Finally, Iran faces significant nationality concerns. Nearly seven million Kurds live in Iran and aspire to their own Kurdish state. A minimum of one-fourth of the Iranian population is Turkic and attracted to Turkey.

PUBLIC DIPLOMACY AND BROADCASTING TO THE MIDDLE EAST

With the end of the Cold War, American interest in public diplomacy waned. The Congress, White House, and State Department no longer considered public diplomacy essential to U.S. national security; consequently, budgets were slashed and reorganizations occurred that weakened the apparatus inherited from the successful struggle with communism. Public diplomacy had become so belittled that by the late 1990s only low-level officials manned the public diplomacy offices within the White House and State Department.

Substantial budget cuts have also weakened the Fulbright Scholars and International Visitors programs that were crucial to our victory in the Cold War. These programs allowed foreign students to study in the United States, and young decisionmakers to visit, providing them with an invaluable opportunity to learn about America first-hand rather than through the distorting lens of foreign media. Reductions in language-training grant programs have led to a dearth of Americans fluent in Arabic and capable of representing the United States on Arab-language television programs. This problem has been further compounded within the United States by the disdain of many academic circles for area studies.

How do we rebuild our public diplomacy apparatus given these glaring weaknesses? We must restore the Cold War public diplomacy apparatus in all its many forms and adapt it to the 21st century. Broadcasting was but one element of a broad-based, global public diplomacy effort that operated in every region of the world. Fulbright scholarships and International Visitor programs should be expanded, despite the difficulties that post–9/11 immigration restrictions have now placed on these programs. Middle East area studies and language programs must be strengthened.

We must also augment our broadcasting efforts. Currently, U.S. budget officials question the need for multiple broadcast instruments within the region: why have an overlap of two radio stations broadcasting to one country when having only one would save money? The lesson of the Cold War is that more broadcast instruments allow for broader audience focus than a single station, thus enabling the United States to reach more mass and elite audiences in a variety of countries. If we are to challenge the terrible misconceptions about the United States that are rampant throughout the Middle East, we must have an effective broadcast capability that will attract differentiated audiences.

Such broadcasts must present news and information in total objectivity. The level of conspiratorial discourse in the Middle East effectively prohibits the use of propagandistic methods; we must entice the populations of the Middle East with fair and balanced news and information (including that which is critical of the United States). Broadcasts must recognize that in reality there is no one "Islamic World" but multiple "Islamic worlds" with widely different cultures and histories. Indeed, many of these societies (for example, the Persians of Iran) date back thousands of years to pre-Islamic times. To succeed we must tailor our messages to these varied groups. We must stress that the values we espouse — democracy, free enterprise, freedom of speech — are universal and not merely Western or American values. Extremist Islamists have very effectively begun to discredit these concepts as purely Western, and not founded in Islamic tradition — although that is not the case. We must support those Middle Eastern scholars brave enough to embrace modernity as an intrinsically Islamic idea.

MEDIA ENVIRONMENT

Successful broadcasting, an essential element of public diplomacy, should both provide a comprehensive view of the United States and promote universal values of tolerance, human rights, and democracy in the region. Under the oversight of the Broadcasting Board of Governors, the United States currently supports a variety of stations that communicate by radio, television, and the Internet to the Islamic World. They include RFE/RL, VOA, and the Middle East Network (Al Hurra Television, Radio Sawa). One radio station (Radio Sawa) and one TV station (Al-Hurra) cover the Arab world. Sawa has a significant audience among younger Arabs, but its information content is necessarily limited by its entertainment format. Al-Hurra is attempting to find an audience in the face of strong competition. The Voice of America Arabic-language radio service has been eliminated and Radio Free Iraq has been downsized. Radio Farda (an RFE/RL-VOA cooperative project), VOA TV, and VOA Persian Service radio reach Iran. These stations also have Internet sites.

Efforts are under way to evaluate the effectiveness of these broadcast media. A series of country Media Survey Reports prepared by InterMedia, an independent nonprofit research organization, help us understand the most effective means of communicating with the Middle East.

Using extensive audience surveys of nearly all countries in that region, InterMedia has compiled data indicating audiences for television (both satellite and local), radio, and the Internet.

These reports conclude that television is the medium of choice in the Middle East—respondents were nearly unanimous in their preference for television as the primary source of news and entertainment. Indeed, possession of a television set is a mark of prosperity, and in Iraq, for instance, one hundred percent of those surveyed claimed that they own one. Ownership of satellite television dishes has dramatically increased in some countries, covering nearly fifty percent of the population. Even in Iran, where satellite dishes are illegal and police regularly fly helicopters to catch those who possess them, satellite television is an extremely popular way for the average Iranian to watch international news programs. (The black market sales of satellite dishes have become so lucrative that the son of a high Iranian government official is reportedly the principal supplier.) Not surprisingly, Al-Jazeera tops the list as the most watched international television station. However, its new competitor, Al-Arabiya, is offering a significant challenge.

Radio has fallen to second place among the preferred methods of gathering news. While the vast majority of the population owns radio sets, their daily use has declined. For instance, when asked what they used "yesterday," only twenty-six percent of Iranians responded with radio, whereas ninety-one percent said they had used television.

Newspaper use is even lower than radio use. In Jordan only ten percent of the population admitted that they used a newspaper "yesterday." In Iran the figure was twenty-four percent, and in Iraq only six percent claimed to read a newspaper on a daily basis.

The survey data indicate that Internet use in the region is still quite limited, often below ten percent of the population. Even in the relatively more advanced Gulf States of Qatar, Bahrain, and the United Arab Emirates, "yesterday" use registered at only six percent of the population.

Consequently, while radio still plays a key role in informing the Islamic worlds, television has become the medium of choice, and Internet use will increase with the spread of personal computers. Media use by decision-makers is more difficult to establish.

Seminar Participants

FOUAD AJAMI. Director of Middle East Studies, Johns Hopkins University

LEONORE ANNENBERG. Director of the Annenberg Foundation Trust

ELENA S. DANIELSON. Director of the Hoover Library and Archives (since retired)

THOMAS A. DINE. President of RFE/RL, Inc.

RICHARD FAIRBANKS. Chairman, Layalina Productions; former Ambassador

JOYCE GARCZYNSKI. Project Coordinator, Annenberg Public Policy Center of the University of Pennsylvania

MATTHEW GUNN. Research Assistant to George P. Shultz

KATHLEEN HALL JAMIESON. Director, Annenberg Public Policy Center of the University of Pennsylvania

A. ROSS JOHNSON. Hoover Fellow; former Director of Radio Free Europe

ANTHONY M. KENNEDY. Justice of the Supreme Court

ABBAS MILANI. Hoover Fellow

NEWTON MINOW Annenberg Professor of Communications, Northwestern University; former Director of the FCC

GREGORY MITROVICH. Conference rapporteur

DAVID NEWTON. Former Director of Radio Free Iraq; former Ambassador to Iraq and Yemen

CHRISTIAN OSTERMANN. Director of the Cold War International History Project, Woodrow Wilson International Center for Scholars

R. EUGENE PARTA. Director of Audience Research and Program Evaluation, RFE/RL, Inc. (since retired)

JOHN RAISIAN. The Tad and Dianne Taube Director of the Hoover Institution

GEORGE P. SHULTZ. The Thomas W. and Susan B. Ford Distinguished Fellow, Hoover Institution

CHARLES Z. WICK. Former director of USIA

APPENDIX B

Cold War International Broadcasting: Lessons Learned

*Briefing to the
Rancho Mirage Seminar*

A. Ross Johnson and R. Eugene Parta

The Cold War Broadcasting Impact Conference, held at Stanford in October 2004 and sponsored by the Hoover Institution and the Cold War International History Project of the Woodrow Wilson International Center for Scholars, reviewed evidence from Western and Communist-era archives and oral history interviews to assess the impact of Western broadcasts to the USSR and Eastern Europe during the Cold War. Conference participants agreed that these broadcasts had an indisputable impact, as documented by external and internal audience surveys, by elite testimony, and by the magnitude of Communist regime countermeasures against the broadcasts. Conference participants then explored the reasons for this impact, drawing on archival data from the target broadcast countries themselves and the experience of veteran broadcasting officials.

INDICATORS OF IMPACT

Audience surveys from among over 150,000 travelers to the West, once-secret internal regime surveys, and retrospective internal surveys commissioned after 1989 all indicated remarkably large, regular audiences to Western broadcasts — about one third of the urban adult Soviet population and closer to a half of East European adult populations after the 1950s. (See Charts 1–6.) These large audiences were further increased by extensive word-of-mouth amplification.

Information conveyed through Western broadcasts was particularly important in influencing attitude and opinion formation during crises. For example, when the USSR shot down the Korean airliner in 1983, Western radio stations immediately reported the incident while Soviet media remained silent for a week. Soviet authorities then launched a major media campaign in an attempt to mobilize Soviet public opinion behind the regime's position that the downing was accidental. By this time, however, many had learned of the incident, and Soviet culpability for it, from Western radio and were highly skeptical of the delayed Soviet media coverage. Outside information was thus more credible than the internal version of events and contributed to shaping alternative attitudes. (See Charts 7–9.)

As another example, Soviet media remained silent on the 1986 Chernobyl nuclear plant disaster until two full days had passed and never provided a full report or necessary health precautions. Instead, Western radio was the first source on the disaster for over a third of Soviets queried in a survey, and it was the most complete source for most. Western radio thus filled the gap when Soviet media was slow and reluctant to report on a major issue. (See Chart 10.)

Other examples of the role of Western radio in contributing to the formation of alternative attitudes, such as the Soviet war in Afghanistan, were presented at the Hoover conference.

Reinforcing this survey data, both Communist and post-Communist elites have testified to the importance of Western broadcasts. Vaclav Havel, in video greetings to the Hoover conference, said that RFE/RL's "influence and significance have been great and profound." Former Hungarian propaganda chief Janos Berecz, in his paper for the conference, said: "I became convinced that Western broadcasts were among the accepted sources of information among the youth." East German spymaster Marcus Wolf, in his memoirs *Man Without a Face,* said "of all the various means used to influence people against the East during the Cold War, I would count [Radio Free Europe] as the most effective."

Another indicator of impact was the massive resources devoted by the Communist regimes to countering Western broadcasts. They organized expensive radio jamming on a massive scale, spending more on jamming than the West did on broadcasting. They placed spies in the Western radios and attempted to interrupt the flow of information to them about domestic developments. They took reprisals against listeners and Radio employees. They organized counterpropaganda, while at the same time secretly circulating monitoring of Western broadcasts among top officials to provide information not available from their own controlled media or intelligence services. Even counterpropaganda had to acknowledge and thus amplify in local media some information provided by Western radios. These countermeasures were a significant drain on domestic resources, yet they failed to neutralize Western broadcasts.

FACTORS OF SUCCESS

How do we explain the remarkable success during the Cold War of these Western information programs that, in national security terms, cost very little? We have identified nine essential elements, which are listed below, not necessarily in order of importance. Our analysis focuses on Radio Free Europe and Radio Liberty, which emphasized saturation home-service "surrogate" programming. The Voice of America (VOA), the British Broadcasting Corporation (BBC), and other Western broadcasters also had significant impact for many of the same reasons.

First, a clear sense of purpose congruent with the aspirations and possibilities of the audiences. We knew what we wanted — to constrain Soviet power (without provoking suicidal revolt), to keep alive hope of a better future, to limit tyranny, and to broaden the boundaries of internal debate, all in order to make the Soviet empire a less formidable adversary. These were long-term, strategic objectives, not short-term policy goals. They emerged after some fumbling in the early 1950s with notions of early "liberation," "rollback," and "keep[ing] the pot boiling."

Second, a capability for sophisticated appraisal of the adversary. Significant Radio resources were devoted — especially at RFE and RL — to detailed analyses of national Communist regimes and the societies they ruled, based on extensive information collection and associated research that drew on Western press, official Communist sources, interviews with travelers, and regime opponents within the target countries. A cadre of specialized researchers was developed with deep area expertise. This information and analysis function was not envisaged at the outset—it was developed at the Radios over time in response to operational need. It became in turn a major input to U.S. government and scholarly analyses.

Third, differentiated and tailored programs for multiple audiences among and within the target countries. RFE and RL were saturation home services with something for everyone (although RL focused more on elites and the urban intelligentsia; RFE more on the general population). Balanced world and regional news was a staple for all audiences. Programs for Communist elites included coverage of conflicts within and among Communist parties and reports on social democracy in Europe. Programs for non-Communist elites covered Western culture and intellectual life and, as internal dissent developed, amplification of that dissent. Programs for general audiences covered everything from agriculture to religion to labor to sports. Banned Western and internal music was featured. Willis Conover of VOA introduced a generation of Russians and Poles to jazz, the RFE Hungarian Service "teenager party" program attracted a generation of Hungarian youth to RFE, and Western music attracted listeners in the other RFE target countries as well. In the USSR, the Magnitizdat phenomenon introduced banned Soviet underground music to a wide public.

Fourth, programs that were purposeful, credible, responsible, and relevant to their audiences. Events of the day were covered, but thematic programming was important as well (e.g., a series on parliamentary institutions in a democracy). Commentary was included along with straight news and news analysis, and audiences were attracted to star-quality commentators. It was essential that programs built and maintained credibility by reporting the bad news along with the good, for example in coverage of Watergate and Vietnam. Responsible programming was (at its best) calm in tone and (after the early 1950s) avoided tactical advice and especially any encouragement of violent resistance. Programming emphasized local developments and was attuned to the listeners through constant audience feedback obtained from traveler surveys and listener mail and through continuous management of quality control.

Fifth, decentralized broadcast organizations. RFE and RL were the models, with autonomous country broadcasting units rather than central scripting. Over the years VOA and BBC moved in this direction as well — and gained larger audiences. Émigré broadcast service directors with intimate knowledge of their audiences, many with prominent reputations, were responsible for broadcast content, within broad policy guidelines and under American management oversight.

Sixth, multi-media operations. Distribution of printed materials supplemented broadcasting in some instances. In the early 1950s, program content was spread in Eastern Europe by balloon leaflets. Subsequently, leaflets, periodicals, Western books, and locally unpublished texts were distributed (by open mail and by travelers) in target countries.

Seventh, appropriate funding and oversight mechanisms. Sufficient public funding was provided by the Congress (although RFE raised some private funds through the Crusade for Freedom). The CIA covertly (until 1971) and then the Board for International Broadcasting overtly (after 1972) made grants to RFE and RL and exercised fiscal oversight, working with the Office of Management and Budget, the Government Accounting Office, and Inspector Generals. The BBC World Service had an analogous relationship to the British Foreign Office.

Eighth, distance from official government policies and journalistic independence. The CIA took a laissez-faire approach to RFE and RL—a relationship insisted on by the Radios' influential boards and CEOs. After 1972 the Board for International Broadcasting (BIB) provided a "firewall" between the Radios and the State Department and other Executive Branch offices. The BIB legislation provided for "an independent broadcast media, operating in a manner not inconsistent with the broad foreign policy objectives of the United States and in accordance with high professional standards," giving RFE and RL considerable journalistic flexibility. Advocacy of specific U.S. policies was not required and, in fact, was avoided. The BBC enjoyed similar autonomy in the British context. VOA's journalistic independence, affirmed in 1976 by law in the VOA Charter, was sometimes challenged by administration policy interference and complicated by the requirement to broadcast administration policy editorials.

Ninth, receptive audiences that identified with many of the goals of the broadcasters. Soviet and East European audiences lived in an "information-poor" environment, were subject to regime propaganda and censorship, and were deprived of other alternative information. East Europeans were artificially cut off from the rest of Europe and were mostly pro-American. Soviet listeners were more under Communist regime influence, but a significant minority were pro-democratic (or at least proto-democratic) in outlook.

CONCLUSION

Western broadcasts had a remarkable impact in the USSR and Eastern Europe in the circumstances of the Cold War.

They reached mass audiences, as documented by traveler surveys at the time and confirmed now by evidence from the formerly closed Communist archives. They reached key elites, both within the Communist regimes and among regime opponents. The keys to the mass and elite audiences were the credibility and relevance of the broadcasts. Government mechanisms were geared to providing public funding and oversight while ensuring management autonomy and journalistic independence.

CHARTS

CHART I
Weekly Reach of Western Radio in Poland: 1962–1988

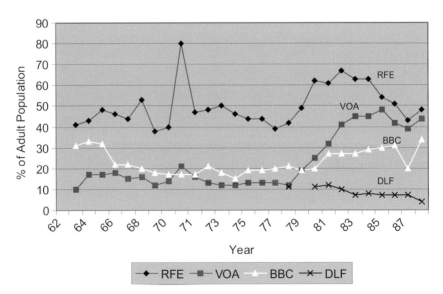

CHART 2

Weekly Reach of Western Radio in Hungary: 1962–1988

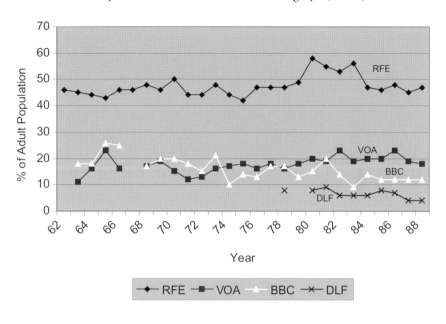

CHART 3

Weekly Reach of Western Radio in Czechoslovakia: 1963–1988

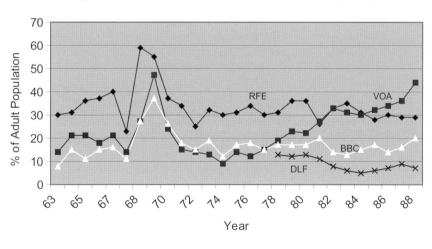

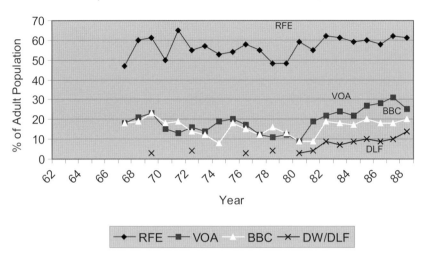

CHART 4

Weekly Reach of Western Radio in Romania: 1962–1988

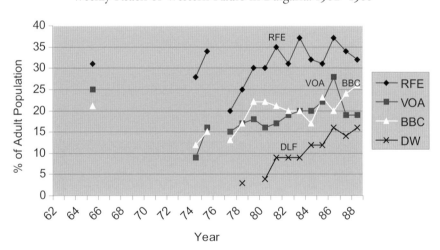

CHART 5

Weekly Reach of Western Radio in Bulgaria: 1962–1988

CHART 6

Weekly Reach of Western Broadcasters in the USSR: 1980–1990

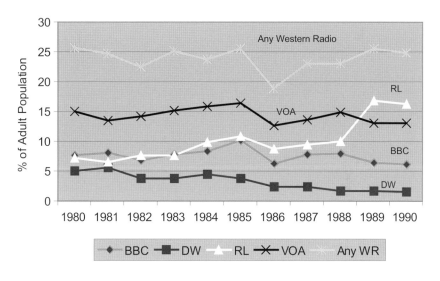

CHART 7

Sources of Information on the KAL Incident

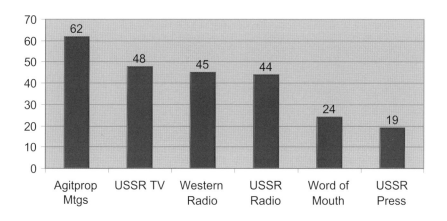

CHART 8

Credibility of Media Sources on KAL Incident Among Listeners and Non-Listeners to Western Radio

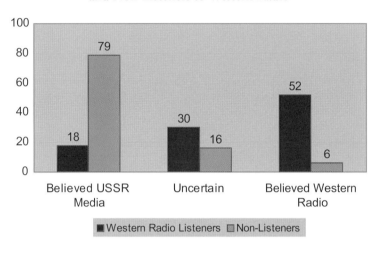

CHART 9

Attitudes Toward the USSR Action in the KAL Incident Among Listeners and Non-Listeners to Western Radio

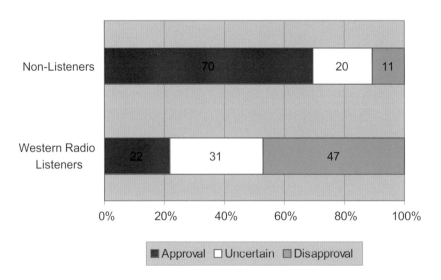

CHART 10

First Source of Information on the Chernobyl Disaster

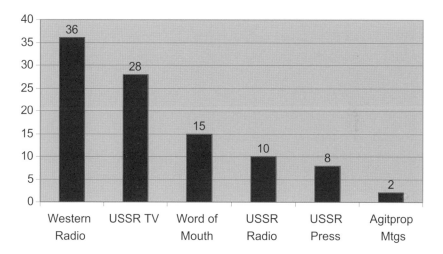

INDEX

alternative information, 13

America. *See* United States

analysis
  communist, 57
  Iranian, 21
  news, 59
  scholarly, 5

anti-Americanism
  breaking down, 40–41
  Middle East, 12, 37
  sources of, 14

Arab Middle East
  dictatorships in, 40
  United States divide from, 11
  See also Pan-Arab nationalists

Arab-Israeli conflict, 13

Al-Arabiya, 17

archives, 9, 62

authoritarianism, 18

Ayatollah, 45

banned media, 58

BBC (British Broadcasting Company), 8, 36

bin Laden, Osama, 38

bloggers, 22

broadcasting
  Cold War, 3
  Communist, viii
  émigré, 35
  independent, 60
  indigenous, 10
  international, 33

broadcasting *(continued)*
  internet, 9
  objectivity, 47
  organizations, 7
  See also western broadcasting
Bulgaria, 64
Bush, George W., 12
  message of, 18
  problematic allies of, 15

capitalism, 21
Cedar Revolution, 31
censorship, 8, 19, 61
Chernobyl information, 67
CIA, 60
clerics, 45
Cold War
  broadcasting, 3
  lessons from, 24
  public diplomacy during, 46
  See also Communist
Cold War International History Project (CWIHP), ix
commentary, 27
Communist
  analysis, 57
  archives, 9, 62
  broadcasting, viii
  regimes, 56
  See also USSR
community

European Muslim, 27
Islamic, 25
virtual, 23
Conover, Willis, 58
counterpropaganda, 56
credibility, 31, 66
culture, 44
Czechoslovakia, 63

debate, 4
democracy
  cost of transition to, 21
  magazines promoting, 22
  Middle Eastern, 16
  spread of, 25
development, 34
dictatorships, 40
diplomacy. *See* public diplomacy

economy, 44
education
  Middle Eastern, 39
  propaganda v., 29
Egypt, 16
  See also Mubarak, Hosni
embargo, 24
émigré(s)
  broadcasting, 35
  exaggeration from, 28
  United States oversight of, 59

European(s)
  East v. West, 61
  Muslims, 3, 27

Fairbanks, Richard, 29
foreign media, 46
foreign policy, 7
fundamentalism, 38

governmental efforts, 29

Hungary
  propaganda of, 55
  western broadcasting in,
    63
Hussein, Saddam, 13, 38

independent broadcasting,
  60
independent journalism, 62
indigenous broadcasting, 10
information
  alternative, 13
  Chernobyl, 67
  KAL incident, 65
  outside v. internal, 55
internal debate, 4
international broadcasting,
  33
internet
  broadcasting, 9

growing presence of, 50
Islamic world on, 48
See also web sites
Iran
  analysis of, 21
  bloggers in, 22
  currant state of, 11
  diaspora media, 23
  domestic picture of, 43
  economy, 44
  embargo on, 24
  newspapers in, 50
  politics in, 20
  public diplomacy in, 41
Iraq
  media culture in, 19
  Shia dominance in, 42
Islam
  community of, 25
  fundamentalism in, 38
  radical, 12
Islamic world
  developments in, vii–viii
  influencing, 24–31
  internet in, 48
  United States communica-
    tion to, 3
Israel, 37

Al Jazeera, 19, 30
John Paul II (pope), 23

journalistic independence, 8, 62

KAL incident
  information on, 65
  USSR action in, 66
Khatami experience, 20

magazines, 22
media, 49–50, 66
  banned, 58
  culture in Iraq, 19
  foreign, 46
  Iranian diaspora, 23
  multi, 60
  of Soviet empire, 54
  strategy, 30
  twenty-first century, 22
Middle East
  anti-Americanism in, 12, 37
  democracy in, 16
  dilemma of, 33
  education in, 39
  propaganda in, 47
  television in, 49
  See also Arab Middle East;
    Arab-Israeli conflict
modernity, 40
Mubarak, Hosni, 15–16
mullahs, 43

multimedia, 60
Muslim(s)
  authoritarianism, 18
  European, 3, 27
  mainstream v. radical, 25
  See also Islam

news
  analysis, 59
  state-controlled, 35
newspapers, 50
9/11, 14, 18, 38
nuclear weapons, 20

oil, 17
organizations
  broadcasting, 7
  research, 48

Pan-Arab nationalists, 39
Poland, 62
policy, 57
politics, 20
private efforts, 29
programming
  Al Jazeera, 30
  responsible, 6
  woman's, 26
propaganda, 8
  education v., 29

of Hungary, 55
in Middle East, 47
regime, 61
Soviet, 34
See also counterpropaganda
public diplomacy
Cold War, 46
Iranian, 41
key elements of, vii
policy/prospects of, 33
United States commitment
to, 36, 45

Al Qaeda, 14

radio, 49–50
Radio Free Europe. *See* RFE
Radio Liberty. *See* RL
regime(s)
Communist, 56
propaganda, 61
research
organizations, 48
survey, 41
revolution, 31, 41
Revolutionary guard, 44
RFE (Radio Free Europe), 5–
6, 36, 48, 58
RL (Radio Liberty), 5, 36, 48,
58

Romania, 64

Saudis
Al-Arabiya owned by, 17
liberal/secularist, 15
scholarly analysis, 5
Security Council, 43
Shia, 42
Shultz, George P., vii
socialism, 39
society, 28
Soviet empire
media of, 54
power of, 4
propaganda, 34
strategy, 4, 30
survey
research, 41
secret, 54
traveler, 62

technological development, 34
television, 49

UN (United Nations), 42
United States
Arab Middle East dividing
from, 11
attitudes toward, vii
culture of, 44

United States *(continued)*
  émigré oversight by, 59
  foreign policy of, 7
  Islamic world communica-
    tion from, 3
  language proficiency in,
    26
  Mullahs checkmate, 43
  pro-Israeli shift in, 37
  public diplomacy commit-
    ment from, 36, 45
  quality control, 35
  values of, 47
  web sites, 10
  worldview of, 28
U.S. *See* United States
USSR
  KAL incident action from,
    66
  western broadcasting in,
    65
  See also Soviet empire

Vietnam, 59
virtual community, 23
VOA (Voice of America), 6, 8,
  36, 48

Wahhabism, 17
Watergate, 59
web sites
  Cold War International His-
    tory Project (CWIHP), ix
  United States, 10
western broadcasting
  in Bulgaria, 64
  countering, 56
  in Czechoslovakia, 63
  in Hungary, 63
  impact of, 53
  in Poland, 62
  in Romania, 64
  success of, vii
  in USSR, 65
  youth accept, 55
  See also radio
woman, 26
worldview, 28

youth
  RFE attraction from, 6
  western broadcasting accepted
    by, 55

al-Zawahiri, Ayman, 14